ABOUT CROWS

The Felix Pollak Prize in Poetry

ABOUT CROWS
CRAIG BLAIS

THE UNIVERSITY OF WISCONSIN PRESS

The University of Wisconsin Press
1930 Monroe Street, 3rd Floor
Madison, Wisconsin 53711-2059
uwpress.wisc.edu

3 Henrietta Street
London WC2E 8LU, England
eurospanbookstore.com

Printed in the United States of America

Library of Congress Cataloging-in-Publication Data

Blais, Craig.
  About crows / Craig Blais.
    p.   cm. — (The Felix Pollak prize in poetry)
  Poems.
  Includes bibliographical references.
  ISBN 978-0-299-29194-5 (pbk. : alk. paper) — ISBN 978-0-299-29193-8 (e-book)
  I. Title. II. Series: Felix Pollak prize in poetry (Series)
  PS3602.L337A64   2013
  811'.6—dc23
                      2012032680

CONTENTS

IV. THE CULT POEM

ACKNOWLEDGMENTS

I gratefully acknowledge the editors of the following publications in which these poems previously appeared, sometimes in earlier versions:

Bateau: "Midwinter Rains over Montréal: A Video Installation"
Bellingham Review: "The Beverly Hills of Korea"
Best New Poets 2007: "Sister at the Airport"
Breathe: 101 Contemporary Odes: "Self-Portrait with Seven Fingers II"
Chiron Review: "Huffers"
Eclipse: "Sister at the Airport"
Good Foot: "Self-Portrait in Shock"
Hayden's Ferry Review: "About Crows"
Mikrokosmos: "Self-Portrait with Seven Fingers I, II, and III"
Nashville Review: "Robert Frost in the Slaughterhouse," "The Rise of Communism"
The Pinch: "Orizuru"
Sentence: A Journal of Prose Poetics: "Scenes from a Village: A Triptych"
Spoon River Poetry Review: "After We Disembark and Spend the Day on the Island while the Ship's Repaired, I Board Alone, Flip through a Chinese Restaurant Calendar, and Write Three Poems to Express My Feelings"

Thank you to Terrance Hayes, Ron Wallace, and everyone at the University of Wisconsin Press.
    Thank you to my workshop professors and classmates at Wichita State University and Florida State University who offered valuable feedback on many of these poems as they were being drafted.
    Thank you to Albert Goldbarth, Rick Mulkey, David Kirby, and John Tierney for friendship, support, and editorial insight; and to Barbara Hamby for helping me see the final shape.
    Lastly, thank you to my family, for a lifetime of encouragement.

I.
THE LOST TOWN

for Melanie

ABOUT CROWS

What kind of shape
would hold this, even briefly, all together,
with no magical bird, and without its song?
LAWRENCE RAAB

(i)

There is always a lone crow high in a tree above a Little League game,
and sometimes one boy, breathing in the oil rubbed into the leather

webbing of his glove, notices it—as he stands alone in left field—and says
nothing about the blue-black darkness on its wing, or this feeling, for

the first time, growing inside of him. He follows the abandoned park
road in the direction of home and searches the limbs breaking the overcast

sky into a puzzle board. For how else could childhood end, if not in slow
and private discovery of this puzzle that will never come together again?

(ii)

Somewhere in this poem, already, I want to use the phrase "a murder
of crows," though I know it's too "poetic" and could only conjure the ghost

of Poe to appear at the margin of this page like a man with his hands
wrapped in bandages among the trees at the edge of a frozen field.

None of the parents seem to mind so long as their children stay in sight;
one now is rounding third—*c'mon, get the lead out!*—as another falls

through the empty space between monkey bars and dirty beach sand.
She brushes away the grains imbedded in her red knees and then looks up

toward the commotion of the foul lines while, from behind, one hand
tightens over her lips as another lifts her tiny body up by the abdomen.

(iii)

When a young crow falls from its roosting perch, both parents fly down
and spend the night on the ground with it. Concern impels them to do this,

as it's difficult to believe they could achieve anything except endangering
their own lives should a fox or another animal discover them in the night.

Carrion crows often come close to man and enable themselves to be shot if
their young cry out in fear, but sometimes the parents simply cannot hear

the plea or the rustling through the dry leaves below, as dark turns toward
a dawn that still-frames the nature scene, and makes it all seem inevitable.

(iv)

In Japan, if a crow flies in a circle three times over your house, there
will be a death in the family. In Japan, the Buddha lives in the larynx;

all sound passing through it should be true. After you die, your family
will sleep in a circle around your casket, and—once the organs and flesh

have burned away from your bones—your loved ones will surround you
again to pick the little visible that remains off the oven tray and place it

in an urn (your body's new shape taking that of the ceremonial vase)
with his Holiness picked up, delicately with chopsticks, last, and set atop

the pile of fragment and ash. After the bones of the throat have been silent
for thirty-nine days, your spirit will be free to leave and enter another body.

(v)

My sister crouches over her coffee table, packing marijuana into a pipe bowl
as a murder of crows reflect off the TV donated by a Christian charity.

My sister has surrendered to her doubt in everything. She won't see doctors
anymore. Uncertain about everything prior to the event: the heart-shaped

chocolate box saved as a keepsake from our father has become—*perhaps*—
a duplicate of the original, bought to replace what she threw away seventeen

years ago. When I tell her I've started to write a book "about crows,"
she says she's not certain if there ever was a bar across the street from her

nursery school or whether watermelons were sold from a truck there
for only a dollar. Though she's been questioned countless times, she's still

unsure what happened before her mouth learned to stop screaming and worked
only to lick condensation from the brick walls of a padlocked root cellar.

(vi)

A raven is simply a famous crow. And though he may have been the most
famous poet of his time, the last five days of Edgar Allan Poe's life are a mystery.

Theories abound, but many believe that after stepping briefly off a boat
bound for Philadelphia from Baltimore, he stopped into a bar for a drink,

where he was kidnapped by political thugs, robbed of his belongings,
stripped of clothes, beaten, drugged, kept in a dark basement overnight,

and then carted with other men, from precinct to precinct, to vote eleven times
in citywide elections. When the night was over, he was left to exposure

in the gutter. The only thing we really know is that when someone finally
came to his aid, it was too late. And nothing he said was comprehensible.

(vii)

A colony of crows surrounds the gun factory every night, flying over
the razor wire to make a living blanket atop the freshly mowed grass

used for company softball games in the summer. The Parks Department
is responsible for what is known as "crow control." It seems odd the city

would hold itself accountable for these birds who, for the most part, roost
on private lands, but it's a job no one else wants; like, until recently,

only the federal government would hand deliver your love letters for
a few cents. To this day, no one's figured a way to turn a profit shooing

thousands of birds from the armory to the roof of the ice hockey rink—
where, inside, children learn to skate on thin blades of sharpened steel.

(viii)

In 1946, A. S. Barnes and Co. published Bert Popowski's *Crow Shooting*—
dedicated to men returning from service overseas, some of whom, because

of wounds suffered in battle, "thought their hunting days were through."
Popowski suggests that counties offer bounties on crows so that game

and songbirds can raise their young in "comparative safety." He says
that every crow hunter carries with him an arsenal of calls, like a pitcher

carries fastball, slider, and curve. There is the call of distress, the call of
discovery, the rallying call, the warning alert and attention call, the casual

"caw-caw-caw" of casual salute, the young crow squall to mother and father
roosting in a distant perch, but hunters only concern themselves with cries

of discovery and distress: calls to attract a flock to a grove of low trees,
where a young corpse dangles from a black cord beneath a plastic hawk.

HUFFERS

The candy aisle smells like gasoline. In the discount grocery, two men in white tank tops
    hold court
in front of the lollipops, debating which sweets little girls like best these days. They pick
    up a bag
and study both sides as if it holds some secret that might seep out from behind the white
    bubble letters.

It's banal, I know, to portray them this way: these two men who, for all we know, have
    committed
no crime besides being stoned and having a sweet tooth (and maybe not even that), and
    anyway,
the evening news said the abductor was a single man: a middle-aged smoker in a white
    sedan
with a red pinstripe along the driver-side door, and perhaps around the entire car, but
    you know

how an early summer morning in the Berkshires feels when you're sixteen in white
    sneakers
wet with dew, engaged in some mindless task, like checking the first aid kit before the
    crowds arrive.
The sun so low in the sky. You wish you could stick out your hand and stop it right there.

SISTER AT THE AIRPORT

On my sister's nights off, she drives alone to the airport and haunts the security gates.
While man, woman, and child wait in line for random screenings, she stands to the side,
     with the other families,
waiting for loved ones to arrive, weary, and smiling, from the other side of the exit doors.
My sister tells me that Western Mass. is all microbrew beer and goodbyes; she prefers to
     be in a place where

people arrive. She tells me, with no sense of shame, that the degree of pleasure she feels is
     contingent
on sex, age, race, and perceived social status. While my sister feels little for the middle-
     class mother
fingering her key ring and car alarm remote in expectation of her son—coming home
from some private university in the South—she's moved to tears at the sight of a child
holding a cardboard sign that reads *WELCOME HOME DADDY*.

My sister has conversations with those standing in wait. No feeling, she says, is so strong
     or pure
as the anticipation of reunion. She listens to their stories and fills with their excitement,
or else excuses herself to go buy coffee. Sometimes my sister tells them she is waiting for
     her boyfriend:
coming home "on leave." Other times, if she doesn't feel like talking, she is there to pick
     up her housemate,
heading back from a business trip. And sometimes she is there to greet me, her brother,

returning from Siem Reap, or some other far off place. When we were younger, she was
responsible for retrieving me from the airport. It was always a red-eye from Oakland,
and everybody else had become bored with homecomings. I am afraid that's when this all
     started.
The whole way home, she could only speak of the people she waited with; as we drove
past the penitentiary, and the fox standing alone in the field of snow beside it, she would
     go on and on.

ROBERT FROST IN THE SLAUGHTERHOUSE

Flies freeze into puddles
beneath the dripping meat hooks
as we maze the swinging,
skinned bodies to the backroom
adjacent the loading docks:
a group of four or five men—
day laborers and a driver—
funnel a steer from a wooden cart
into the "jaws of death."
Hind legs quickly roped,
the beast is pulleyed into the air,
where they cut its throat
and drain the warm blood
into a pail held by a young boy,
almost my age, dancing
perilously beneath.
All afternoon Father drinks
cup after cup to cure the sickness
that has settled in his lungs,
and by the time we squint out
into the sun, my jaw
is numb—though the fog
has lifted one more day
off the distant hills
of Sausalito and Marin.

SUBURBAN MYTHOPOETICS

After the kid next door lost both eyes to cancer,
echolocation helped detect the objects around him.
Acrylic prosthetics are like dead stars, I think, as I sit
on the front porch watching him glide on his bike
around the cul-de-sac—tongue-clicking sound waves
off Saturns, station wagons, and even my grandfather

after losing so much, retained the *I'm falling* feeling
just before his hip crashed the cellar floor.
Spatial memory and sense of motion, the doctor
explained, are usually last to go. This might be why
he was down there building birdhouses
in the first place: because classical sailors were kiss-asses

of the high seas, their simple plan to keep from sinking
to the wine-dark deeps involved carving
the Gemini twins into the bows of their ships
in hopes of flattering safe passage. It was common
wisdom that if one became cloud-covered, they were
meeting some tragedy, like Somali pirates

launching grenades at a Disney cruise ship—
who do those crews pray to? And who should I call on
to protect the miniature golf course and medical clinics
stockpiled with sunblock and Dramamine
when terrorists aim pontoon planes full of gasoline
at one of three rotating four-star restaurants? My grandfather

is pissed. He's telling me, when he comes for the dog,
about the loss of hearing in his right ear. And the quack
who checks his brains keeps making moves on him.
It's always: *What's your name? Where do you live?*
What do you like to do in your free time? To which he replies,
every time, *Listen, I love my wife.* My grandfather is pissed

and telling me again about his hearing when he returns
with the dog, because I'm not doing anything, just writing
a plane out of the sky from the front porch. Because

I put it there. And because I was born in June. And because
someone has to protect the 8,000 gallons of Neapolitan
ice cream and the numb hands that do the scooping.

My grandfather opens the car door as my neighbor leans
his bike against a fire hydrant (or mailbox?) and tongue-clicks
a sound wave off him. I think they couldn't possibly
have anything to say to each other. But each acknowledges
the other—the presence of something—when the car's put in gear,
and sweat drips into my neighbor's wide, unblinking eyes.

AN ALTERNATE HISTORY OF ENFIELD, MASS.

(i)

"I wanted you to rape me," she said, remembering our walks behind her prep school
    dorm,
the damp leaves plastered to soil and stone on the path beside the stream, the land bridge
leading to an abandoned logging road that climbed out of the ravine, the fieldstone
    foundation
of an old farmhouse littered with beer cans and graffiti. Warped plywood over an empty
    cellar hole.

She: all solid muscle and soft skin. Four tiny scars on one knee from where the screws
    were tightened,
then forgotten. She couldn't have known her touch would have turned me into smoke.
Seized by stupidity, I didn't know she desired rapture at fourteen, as I held out for
a storybook glade that never appeared, only shattered branches and contorted limbs.

I still don't know if light or wind twists them that way, or why the red pines—growing
at equal distance and height around the reservoir—point toward the white sky in rows.
A brick chimney breaches cloud-covered water, in a light that's less like light than feeling,
because there's no source to be found. Old-timers say brown trout nest in the potholed
    roads below.

(ii)

Enfield isn't a town in Western Mass. Enfield no longer exists. Disincorporated and
    flooded
eighty years ago to meet demands for water in Boston, its residents were annexed to the
    hill towns
of New Salem, Belchertown, Pelham, and Ware. It wouldn't have worked just anywhere.
Engineers needed a place where the rolling hills created a bowl. To make the Quabbin

all it took was one dike and a dam to hold four hundred billion gallons. And then came
the "woodpeckers," out-of-work Bostonians promised jobs by the governor in the last
    election.
They moved through the area like prison work crews, clearing trees below the intended
    shoreline,
leaving mountaintops untouched as future islands. At night, while the remaining men
    headed

to the last bar, these tourists paced through the dark five feet apart, planting saplings
of spruce, red pine, and larch. The horizon range glowed onto the west branch of Swift
    River
as it overflowed into Rattlesnake Den and Bobbin Hollow, pooled in rows of tobacco,
filled the charred basements of wrecked homes, and brimmed over all the emptied
    graves.

(iii)

When the handful of "Lost Towners" gather at the Visitor's Center to recall their
    childhoods
in the valley, they agree the anger's almost gone. All Robert Wilder's family got was $1,500
for forty acres, a couple barns, and a farmhouse. His grandfather bitched the timber alone
was worth $5,000, but no one listened. He turned to moonshining and held on until
    forced out.

Bob Johnston moans that he's the only one left who remembers trout fishing West Branch.
His earliest memory is watching his father hook a baby field mouse, pink and hairless,
through the back of the neck and toss it into the rising stream. A two-pounder jumped—
its rust-colored jaw exposed to morning light—and grabbed the hook midair.

"The girls were made to stay indoors," says Bunny Beardsley. "There were convicts among
    them;
they'd sleep under the brush to get out of work. A couple local girls married engineers,
and a couple just disappeared. The younger ones, like us, didn't know a farm couldn't
    just be moved.
We all thought we were being forced from our homes, into some great adventure."

(iv)

The bodies are buried randomly. No attempt was made to reinter them according to their
    original layout.
It's by accident that we even happen down the dirt road circling the grassy mounds.
We've stopped talking now. All I can think about is silence, the scent of patchouli,
how long I should wait to pull another Camel Wide from our shared cigarette pack.

Peroxided hair chopped at the jawbone. I decided to put her in her school skirt, so it
    would be easy
for you to imagine me grabbing her waist from behind and forcing her quietly down to
    the ground.
The moss slowly bleeding through her thin blue sweater, plastering my jeans to my
    knees.

Fear can't be the only thing to keep this memory from being real. Fear can't be the only
    reason

there's no postcard New England town in the valley below us, with a welcome sign that
    reads
something like "Saved by the Water Riots of 1930," when my overcautious body
presses hers into the bone-filled earth, and she looks right through me, as I stare into her
light blue eyes and wonder what bird she's watching bounce in the black branches above.

When I read the narratives and lyrics—the odes, meditations, epistolaries, postcards,
  prayers, pastorals, elegies, *testimonios*, ballads, and fragments,
when I considered sound, form, rhythm, syntax, symbolism, structure, metaphor,
  diction, tone, style, image, and line,
how soon I grew underwhelmed by the poems themselves and found myself turning to
  the perfect silence of the biographies
about poets forced to suffer in distant prisons, to take foreign names, to translate agony
  into alien tongues,
about poets with parentheses beside their names: (1912–?),
about poets who didn't die but disappeared into the North,
whose last words were found stitched into the lining of a coat three months after falling
  from a death march,
whose last words were recovered from mass graves and dried in the sun,
whose last words were pressed with fingernails into a bar of soap,
how soon I found myself replacing their words,
so that "Golden tones of sunset" became "kidnapped and presumed dead,"
so that "Raindrops on a mulberry leaf" became "solitary confinement for three years,"
so that "The time for you to come is the time when I am waiting" became "possible victim
  of medical experimentation,"
O chiming city!
O atrocity!
O gulag moon glow waterboarding winter orchid O harbor boat torturer O O secret police!
how soon I wanted to close the book and wander off alone—without wallet, pen, paper,
  keys, or cellphone—into the dark swamps around my house,
until I was knee-deep in the rushes and lost completely,
until I could only think of myself desperate for safety,
until I could look up and see: no stars.

THE FALL OF COMMUNISM

(i)

Nobody fakes their own death anymore. When I was a kid it happened
all the time. One day someone was with you, and the next, gone.

Elvis was routinely spotted pumping gas, and Jim Morrison was alive
somewhere in Africa, training a child army for a coup that never

came to pass. Once, I was lifted out of bed in the middle of the night
and forced by my father to walk a block and a half in my pajamas;

a three-family on the edge of the park was on fire. I don't recall
smoke or flames. What I remember is the blue lights of a parked

police cruiser scanning the faces of neighbors I'd never seen
like a copy machine. But there were fires on TV, and I knew

no one recovered from them. The inside of the house was probably
charred clean; and the family, I thought, must have leapt to their deaths.

(ii)

When my brother returned from Germany, he brought with him
the Berlin Wall. There's a picture of him somewhere, going at it

with a pickaxe. And another of him smiling in a field of bone chips.
But he was sixteen, so all he talked about were the prostitutes.

(iii)

After my father's factory closed and we stopped bringing his lunch
down to the river in the afternoon, I learned it had really just moved

to South Carolina, then Mexico, and then China, and by summer's end,
as we walked down the graffitied road to the baseball fields, the house

had risen anew—repaired, whitewashed, and smelling of warm bath towels.
Nothing, and no one, it turned out, ever really died. My brother and I

would never have to drink forties in the park before a morning burial
while Puerto Rican kids rode stripped bikes down a pine-needled path

and launched off plywood and milk crate ramps into the water—
the surface algae spreading briefly, then sealing around their necks.

The thin slate gravestones around town were only artifacts of something
that happened a long time ago, but, luckily, had been defeated.

(iv)

Spray-painted red and green on one side, and a hundred times the size
of the square-inch fragments sold at K-Mart with scrolls of authenticity,

my father appeared grateful when my brother hoisted it from his bag,
but we all remembered him asking for a brick from the ovens.

THE HISTORY OF HOCKEY IN MY TOWN

I don't know how fast he was driving that Friday night; and, no, I don't know the year.
It was after "Old-Time Hockey" Eddie Shore reacquired the franchise, renamed it the
    Indians,
and dropped the first puck wearing a flowing feathered headdress. After a one-year stint
    by the New England Whalers,
captained by a gray-haired Gordie "Mr. Hockey" Howe, who briefly brought to town the
    Howe Hat Trick:
awarded to any player who could boast a goal, an assist, and a fight in a single night.

It was years after the Indians moved to their own new home: another staid civic center
meant to revive a downtown in a depression men on ice couldn't rescue it from.
Like any local historian, I can tell you what the event followed, and I know what it
    preceded.
I can plot the car ride on a timeline and fix it between all we agree on as "certain."

It was before the PVC piping below the ice surface clogged with the residue of cold
    ammonia
for the last time, and no one had the funding (or cared enough) to replace it.
Before games gave way to trade shows, county fairs, and the annual Shriner's circus.
Before the Hartford Whalers took the name of a natural disaster and relocated
to North Carolina, to capture the Stanley Cup that had eluded them up north.

When high school hockey games were the only ones played at the Eastern States Coliseum
and draft beers were fifty cents a cup. And a few men who still remembered
nights of standing-room-only, when coaches played, came to sway in the wooden
    bleachers
and spiral into the deep spell of melancholy some mistake for wisdom, repeating to
    themselves
all night, something like: *We built the walls because we loved the space inside.*

When one of those men stood you heard peanut shells no longer swept after each game
crack beneath their boots, and when one of them put his hand on the shoulder . . .
No, one knew better than to put his hand on the shoulder of the man staggering forward
    and back, trying to bundle
three boys in winter coats before stumbling toward the station wagon in the parking lot.

One knew better than to look at him too long in the face, or to say anything besides *See
    ya.*

Like any local historian, I've deduced the points in both time and space. Between the coliseum
and our home on Hungry Hill, that night my father took the merge sign on the I-291
        on-ramp
too literally and drove onto the median to bend it—suddenly—off our front windshield:

a single moment in the history of hockey in my town. Eddie Shore, Marcel Paille, Brian
        Kilrea.
Gordie Howe and his sons Mark and Marty. Eddie Shore again. The Indians, Kings,
        Whalers,
Indians again, and finally, a cartoon Falcon. A secret pact among men in a dark driveway:
some nigger must have smashed it in with a baseball bat while we were inside cheering
        for overtime.

FIVE MEMORIES OF MOTION

(i)

My father didn't want us delivering in our own neighborhood.
It was fine when my middle brother had a starter route:

thirty papers on our street and a couple more spilling around
the block; he didn't have to cross any busy streets,

and the whole thing could be completed in fifteen minutes.
But when you bumped up to four or five hundred,

neighbors were bound to catch wind that delivering
had become the family business. At eight, I could only think

he was trying to protect us from embarrassment. The same way
I took him at his word when he brought the family dog

to the pound after it leapt the fence and bit the Shriner's clown
up the street, and came back claiming that when he got there

he met a guy who said, "Sebastian'd be perfect for my gas station
in the country!" It never occurred to me he would lie, just as

it never occurred shame still rattled around inside men
at thirty-nine, that the half-drunk man with ink-stained hands

who stumbled in our kitchen at night, mumbling maxims
on work, would grow silent in the car crawling through the projects

at dawn, as we ran from door-to-door-to-tailgate, and he listened
to the police scanner like he was awaiting the voice of God.

(ii)

The local news is closing with a "feel good" on the nine-year-old
neighbor. He can't see but he's a genius of sorts, compensating

for his blindness with his sense of motion. The theme
is tolerance and overcoming adversity. There's a clip of him

whacking a ball off a tee and dashing up the first-base path
while the rest of his fourth grade class stand frozen in smiles

for the camera. My experience is that he can dodge a tag
if you trap him in a pickle, but these kids don't put forth

any effort. When my sister's smoking hand hovers left,
and gently rolls the ash from her joint against the smooth

inside of the glass ashtray, she doesn't take her eyes
off the show. They say this sense is primal and in us all—

one of the lesser known outside "the big five"—like stretch
receptors in our lungs. Some foundation just gave

my neighbor a scholarship to a state college, and after the next
commercial break, they'll reveal the home renovations

volunteers completed to make life easier: an open-plan
kitchen with motion-sensor faucets, a spaceship bed,

and the parents' new master suite, with cornflower blue
walls so fresh, the boy says he can smell the wet paint.

(iii)

Proprioception: the seventh sense. My sister researches it.
Unconscious awareness of movement arising from stimuli

within the body. Hypothesized by neurophysiologist
Sir Charles Scott Sherrington, the same year that claimed

the first known victim of Alzheimer's: 1906. She's reading
about that too. Of Auguste Deter, Dr. Alzheimer wrote:

"At lunch she eats cauliflower and pork. Asked what
she is eating she answers *spinach*. Asked to write

Auguste D., she tries to write *Mrs.* and forgets the rest."
When the Exelon patch kicks in maybe he can drive again,

my sister suggests, as my grandfather walks the dog
out front. But she hasn't read *his* medical reports,

which recommend we place an anonymous call to police
and have his license taken away. He says he's been doing it

since he was fourteen, driving around Dover, New Hampshire,
during the war, while his brother made it with lonely girls

in the backseat, and he's *not . . . stopping . . . now*. Before grabbing
his hat and heading toward the driveway to leave, he slowly

takes a knife out from his coat pocket, and from a rumpled
sandwich bag, slices a doggie treat into razor-thin wafers.

(iv)

After my parents retrieved my sister from the police station
in the summer of '88, after she'd been observed and evaluated

by experts, and finally released, nothing happened. Life went on
just as it was before the abduction. And sometimes,

when watching my older brothers throw her around
the swimming pool, with bright orange floaties blown up

around her biceps and her screaming mouth revealing
the same missing teeth as any other kid her age,

I'd ask myself, Did she ever *really* go missing? Wasn't she
just away at camp last summer? But then my parents,

or grandparents, or an aunt or uncle, would speak
with their heads lowered at the kitchen table,

in hushed tones, to some new stranger—a distant relative
or investigator—about the place where she'd been found,

the black hole in the ground that had been pried open
and she'd been pulled out of, and I'd feel the need to

go into the living room just to be closer to her, to sit
on the couch beside her and watch TV. Each cushion

is an island, I would tell her, and the ground is lava.
If you don't want to burn to death, don't move.

(v)

When my father died I was running laps around the hospital.
My grandfather was the only one he wanted in the room

with him—because he wasn't his own father but his in-law
and best friend. We had good times, my grandfather

tells me and my sister with a look of pity in his eyes
that says he thinks we haven't. Then he launches into

his second favorite driving story, the one where he and my dad
leave the hockey game at Eastern States Coliseum and drive

drunk down to the porno theater in Enfield, Connecticut,
while my father smokes a joint in the passenger seat.

This one ends with the broad on the big screen deep-throating
the star, and my father saying *something* that got

the whole place roaring. *I don't remember what*, my grandfather
confesses, but I know five minutes later he was passed out

in his seat. The story always ends there. He leaves out
the drive home—a straight shot north—guided by the river

and sound barriers, the swing sets rusting beyond. The highway
empty, windows cracked. My father liked to close his eyes

for just a moment at times like that, to trust all our lives
to that movement, as he pushed the smoke from his lungs.

II.
THE BEVERLY HILLS OF KOREA
(OR, MY LIFE IN THE
LOVE MOTEL)

THE BEVERLY HILLS OF KOREA

(i)

Although the apple travels a greater distance, we know the earth
rises ever so slightly to meet it. And though the green tea

with honey the waitress has placed on the table at the psychic café
will cool as the fortune-teller flips through onionskin pages to find

my girlfriend's Chinese sign, birth date, and time, the room, too,
will warm, and humidify infinitesimally.

(ii)

If Whitman left New York on a train heading west, and didn't circle
around at the Rockies but hopped a Pacific freighter straight;

and if Cendrars left Montmartre on a train heading east—say
he picked up an assistantship with a pocket watch salesman

and befriended a ditzy prostitute along the way—
who do you think would arrive first in the Beverly Hills of Korea?

(iii)

The knife-sharpener? Or the cobbler? We know they are one-
and-the-same when we see the old man pedaling

his upside-down bicycle frame, turning the stone wheel and sharpening
the sushi chef's blades. Sparks lob across the busy sidewalk

in front of our officetel twice a month, lengthening the line
of housewives: their heelless pumps and dull cleavers in hand.

(iv)

Sometimes the same elements that make up our bodies collapse
into an area smaller than the region can hold

and gravity draws everything, hopelessly, toward it. Not even
light escapes. We know the Beverly Hills of Korea acts the same way.

Our error was assuming Whitman and Cendrars had a choice,
their vessels barreling toward us.

(v)

Although the traveling cobbler/knife-sharpener set up shop
on our sidewalk twice a month, the sushi chef's wife asked me

to the Hills to fix a strap on her taupe sandals. And though I knew
my girlfriend would be in the same neighborhood, getting her fortune read

with friends, I crowded under one umbrella with my neighbor
and let her hand snake around my bicep like we had no choice.

(vi)

Because circumstance made us aficionados of love motels—of rooms
with swings, Edward VII chairs, Jacuzzis, and mechanical sex beds.

Because we'd learned which back muscles to tighten and to loosen
hips as moans marked the automated mattress like a metronome.

Because on tiptoes we unscrewed red light bulbs, as the BBC reached
out from the next room—something about a subway attack in London.

(vii)

If Blaise refuses to leave Little Jeanne behind at an unnamed station,
would Walt then find an excuse to drag along Peter Doyle?

(But O! I can only see Whitman traveling alone.)
Perhaps making eyes at the youth across the aisle, but finally

deciding to take his newly sharpened paring knife from his coat pocket
to nimbly skin and split a Macintosh apple and offer him half.

(viii)

When you enter the tunnel, the flicker of light behind your eyelids
tricks you into thinking the whole car is up in flames.

Because fire in dream is both fear and desire, it forces you from home
then burns as the light that leads you back again.

The shoe slips from the foot of your neighbor now slouched against you
and the steel wheels rise slightly off the tracks to meet it.

(iv)

It is fractal in nature: these two women's lives intersecting
at a larger point of crossing, a transfer stop where I might

have disappeared in any direction. But too far from home,
I stayed, if only to listen to the chorus of disbelief rising. Music

that draws one in, like the old man in a felt hat toward the younger—
with his suitcase full of counterfeit watches.

ALL THE SIGNS READ 어서 오세요

But you and I walk away from the lights,
down concrete steps that disappear into the yield of sand beneath our feet—the entire
     ocean falling
from the shore—to lay out a blanket on the beach for a midnight picnic of grilled squid
     and whiskey.

Through charcoal smoke, you sing a song you've been rehearsing with the mothers' choir,
then say something about the sulfur in a match-head affecting the taste of your cigarette,
     and

lastly, like some conspirator sharing secrets in the dark, you tell me the three things you
     no longer
believe: one, the government is bullshit; two, true love is a myth; and three, God doesn't
     exist.

So, when we carry the things back to the love motel, and you enter the bathroom to
     shower
the sand and sea from your skin, I follow you in. Your only condition is that we turn off
     the lights.

A RIVER[1]

The countryside:
        in a café overlooking
           a river: through a windowpane
      dripping with beads of rainwater:

a red speedboat circles back
        to retrieve a lost ski[2]
                as she tells me
    about the dead
         and how they're buried.
She doesn't know
        nothing
interests me more.[3]

        The booth is private—the way
      she likes it—
so the waiter has to
        clear his throat
        before pushing through
               the curtained doorway
      with another refill
         of the house special
     and hazelnut coffee.
When chain-smoking
            every moment
        becomes private to me.

      She says her husband
        owns a mountain.[4]

---

[1] Or, *About Cows*.[a]

[2] Two things: I know it's strange that people should be waterskiing in the rain. But the thing is, it was a beautiful day right up until then. And second, a cow lying down in a pasture is not necessarily a sign of rain.[b]

[3] 70 percent of my poems are about death and/or dying. The other 30 percent are about cows.

[4] 70 percent of Korea is mountains, which many people proudly translate as "uninhabitable."[c]

    [a] Or, *The Other River*.

    [b] It wasn't like a frozen river in Washington State, where a young woman, whom I will call Sue 1, and her friend, whom I will call Sue 2, walked together at 2:30 a.m. with a bottle of Boone's Strawberry Wine wrapped tight inside a barn coat. Sue 2 reports that Sue 1 started stomping on the edge of the river, shouting, "Under the frozen river the other river flows . . . on its side in the dark!" until her boot broke through the first river and sunk into the second, soaking her foot in the icy water. Sue 1 and Sue 2 were three miles from home.

    [c] There is only one place that is completely uninhabitable: the utility room in Dr. E's townhouse in Chicago, Illinois. When he goes in there, he duct tapes the edges of the door and hangs a quilt to block any trace of light. After thirty minutes, he begins to see the molecules inside his eyes breaking down, emitting photons, which, he says, "can only be compared to fireworks." This is "the dark light of the eye"—the end of seeing.

His father is buried there
                    and his mother will be too.
            She, her husband,
        and our son
will share one tomb,   and because of shortages
            in land,
                    they'll be cremated,
                    placed in urns,
        and stacked on top of each other.

                    I've seen them on the side
            of the highway—
                            grass-covered mounds
grazed by family cattle,
                with modest stone
            monuments
            stating name, date of birth,
                            and death—

                and nothing like
        whatever   one might imagine
            by listening to her.[5]

When I was ten
            my mother bought me
                    a burial plot.[6]
        She said she wanted everyone
                        to be together   forever,
            so she got a group of twelve
in the front row
            of St. Rose de Lima[7]

---

[5] I think she's confusing *mound*, *mountain*, and *monument*, which despite their phonic similarities all have distinct etymologies. *Mound* is from Old English, meaning "a fence or hedge" (any kind of barrier, really, to keep in sheep or cows), while *mountain* comes from Old French by way of the Latin *montanea* (like the state), and *monument* is from Middle English via Latin for "a reminder." This happens a lot, where she comes really close to the intended, appropriate word but shoots just off the mark, creating a completely unintended meaning, like when she asks me about the book I'm working on, "About Cows," no matter how many times I correct her: "It's *About Crows*."

[6] She was buying one anyway, and it was cheaper in bulk. When I asked my mother about it on the phone, she said, "It was something like $400 for two, $600 for four, and $1,200 for, you know, the largest option."

[7] The first American saint. Born in Lima, Peru, in 1586, she disfigured her own face with pepper and lye in order to deter suitors and protect her virginity. She slept on a bed of broken glass, stone, potsherds, and thorns. She was known mainly for her exquisite lacework. The first cow arrived in the Americas, in Jamestown, Virginia, when Rose was twenty-five. I don't know when the first cow arrived in Peru.[d]

[d] Billy G. from Kansas City, Missouri, was only twenty-four when he woke up in his best friend's guestroom covered in his own blood and vomit. "Don't worry about it," his best friend said as he threw the sheets and his mother's lace bedspread into the washing machine. Billy's friend wanted to go to the lake to sell T-shirts. It was then that Billy G. stopped worrying so much about what happened during his blackouts and started wondering instead who would find him, how long would it take, what shape he'd be in, and what the person would do with him after he was dead.

30

in Chicopee, Massachusetts.
It, too,
has a highway going by it.[8]

---

[8] I want to be buried where I die. And I hope that's not Chicopee. I like the idea that if someone wants to pay their respects they need to travel to the place where a person last lived. Like Butch Cassidy and the Sundance Kid, how beautiful and weird that a couple American boys, from Pennsylvania and Utah, respectively, should be buried in Bolivia.[e]

> [e] But maybe that's just not the French-Canadian way. Jack K. from Lowell, Massachusetts, for instance, died in St. Petersburg, Florida, from complications related to alcoholism, esophageal hemorrhaging (he was vomiting blood). But his wife Stella didn't bury him in Florida—*and* she ignored his request to be interred in Nashua, New Hampshire, next to his father and brother; instead, she buried him in her family's plot at Edson Cemetery in Lowell. What say did he have in the matter? For this reason, I think my final resting place is likely to be in Chicopee, even if I die in a seedy motel in Seoul.[1]
>
> ---
>
> [1] Or, *My Blackouts Are Darker than Your Blackouts.*
> At this time I was living in a "love motel" in the Moran neighborhood in the outer suburbs of Seoul. The principal of the school where I worked, the one in the café with me overlooking a river, arranged for me to stay there. She knew the manager, and my suspicion is that she received a cut from the rent I paid. Each room in the motel had a theme: there was the Mongolia Room, the Disney Room, the Classroom Room, the Hello Kitty Room, the Subway Car Room, etc. But because particular rooms were reserved for certain nights, I was shuffled around the motel depending on vacancy. Often I'd come home from drinking after work and—in the midst of a blackout—would be escorted to an available room by someone at the front desk. I'd wake up on the operating table in the Emergency Room Room, with an IV bag of lube hanging from the metal rack beside me.
> I knew then I'd never know what happened the night before—Why were my boots wet? Was I right to remember fireworks? And why was the bedspread covered in brown blood? The last thing I'd remember was looking back and seeing my ghost on all fours, wiping clean the urine spots around a public toilet. And there would be a ghost behind my ghost—paler and more transparent—rubbing away the smudges left on the tile by my ghost's sweaty knees. And a ghost behind my ghost's ghost collecting stray hairs from the crotches of pine trees.
> So I stopped the detective work and came up instead with a formula to determine how long it would take for my mother to put my body in the ground in Chicopee, Massachusetts.
> 1. The time it would take for a couple to request the room I died in: 1–5 days, depending on chance and the day of the week.
> 2. The time it'd take for the front desk to contact my work and/or the police: +1 day.
> 3. The time it'd take before my work and/or the police contacted immigration and found an emergency contact number in my alien registration file: +1 or 2 days.
> 4. The time it'd take for my mother to contact the U.S. Embassy + the time it'd take for them to arrange for my body to be transported home: 3 days?
> 5. Travel time: +1 day.
> 6. Autopsy: +1 or 2 days.
> 7. Wake and funeral arrangements: +2 or 3 days.
> It would take ten to seventeen days for my body to get from the love motel to the front row of St. Rose de Lima.
>
> ---
>
> Bury half of me in Bolivia and half of me in Peru.

THE RISE OF COMMUNISM

The first night, I thought stray dogs were fucking in the streets.
But after leaving the motel in the morning, I saw a pit bull
circling in a small wire cage next to the coffee vending machines.

White is the color of mourning, the cheeks of tree sparrows
in branches on Tiananmen Square's border, the long line of tourist
T-shirts twisting away from the Mao Zedong Mausoleum, the lies

about undercover agents eavesdropping on conversations
commonsense says happen far from where the chairman stews
in formaldehyde against his dying wish. Signs in nine languages

but not one mention of the intern who, when pushing embalming
bloat from the dead man's face into his neck, broke off a piece
of his right cheek and replaced it with makeup and Vaseline.

Three paragraphs on the vacuum-sealed crystal casket, and not a word
about the heart and bladder floating in mason jars in the basement.
"It smells like Graceland," whispers the man behind me in line

as we file up the narrow stairs and exit through the gift shop.
Maybe we place the dead behind glass in an attempt to reflect
our own images back at ourselves, on top of someone else, because

we long to fall into the body of a stranger like the lost child
in the woods falls asleep beneath the twisting limbs of an elm.
The sale of death is like the sale of sex, like the massage parlors

across from the motel, where on the second night I learn the crowd
gathers in the florescent glow of the display windows to watch
one dog lock its jaws into the snout of another, while the showcased

girls sit cross-legged in white boxes on the linoleum floor, slurping
instant noodles from Styrofoam bowls. The death whine is heard
for blocks around when it rises from deep in the bait dog's belly.

MONGOLIA ROOM

(i)

She sits cross-legged in a felt yurt with a fake fire
in the center, fixing her hair in the hand-held mirror
she took from the apartment I abandoned.

I couldn't have raised a child with her anyway;
I've grown too used to her telling me it's time to leave.
That, and she's twelve years older than me.

We share the sign of the horse, which might explain
her love of Room 39, and her love of Mongolia,
where humans are outnumbered twelve to one.

"I don't know when my husband will return!
He's on a raid! I'm hungry, angry, lonely,
and tired! I'm trying to warm myself by the fire!"

(ii)

The lobby and front desk are below us. We hear
the front door bells clanging the comings
and goings of high school couples and call girls.

She was thirty-nine when we first met, a number after
my father's death that always found its way onto
bike locks, credit cards, and lottery tickets, and an age

I had always thought impossible to approach—the way
father turns to older brother, then friend, until finally,
the hard luck blossoms and he becomes

someone younger: a nephew, or a son. I started
to look for others who by getting there before me
might show the way. But still, the first time we fucked

(iii)

it all of a sudden struck me: *She's thirty-nine*,
and I had to remind myself that age is just
a number, and you can't make love to a number.

"Genghis Khan was buried somewhere near here!"
she shouts while painting windburn on her cheeks.
"Somewhere near the Onon River!" They say

the funeral party destroyed every living thing in its path,
and after the body was buried, servants stampeded
thirty-nine teams of thirty-nine horses each

over the burial grounds. The servants were then massacred
by soldiers, who in turn were slaughtered on their way home.
For miles around, riderless horses trampled corpses

(iv)
                    on the bloodied steppe. Clouds spread.
                                  The dark parts of the sky grew darker,
until the moon reflected light onto a part of the earth that reflected nothing

               of the simple, single-minded man hidden within it.
            Then he entered legend.
             A name some people
                                      sometimes repeated

to evoke their vague ideas on grief, ambition,
                                        whatever.
                      "I just came back from marmot hunting!"

                                His grave his final victory—
not a slightly sunken plot of dead grass in an ugly field
                                    (like most of ours will

be)
            but an entire country.
                    Any place a family sets up camp tonight
        might be directly above his remains.

(v)
Varnished logs glued together to teepee the fire's guts.
Red and yellow lights pointed at a crinkled aluminum
cylinder spun by a small electric motor.

"They don't really burn wood!" she yells while fastening
the clasps on the shoulder of her *deel*. "There aren't enough
trees! The stoves are fueled by dried yak feces!"

Without breaking a single bone, a skeleton can be divided
into 206 pieces, not thirty-nine. Each needs
protection from altars and national museums, protection

from display cases with motion sensors and humidity
gauges. Each needs to be guarded from becoming a charm
in some kid's pocket he nervously rubs his thumb against.

(vi)

Because that's—"Almost ready!"—what happens
to the material world. The thing acts on our consciousness
or our consciousness acts on the thing. It doesn't matter

which. Maybe both. Train tickets, phone numbers, amphi-
theater seats, even women who take the hand-held
mirrors from the apartments we abandon, are the dead

speaking to us, or our consciousness entering the world
like a foot sliding into a pointy-toed riding boot
as we stand just outside a tent, listening—"Okay!"—

for our cue, to press play on the stereo and forcibly enter
while the fake stone speakers drown out mock screams
with the sound of 1,521 stampeding horses.

III.
THE ERROR GALLERY

SELF-PORTRAIT WITH SEVEN FINGERS I

For me a painting is a surface covered with objects depicted in a certain order. For example, the headless woman, who, with a milk pail, figures on this canvas—if I had the idea of separating her head from her body it was because I needed a space just at that spot.

MARC CHAGALL

I struggle to make room for you, Chagall, to let your childhood meld with mine, to imagine,
as I would have as a child, that your work steps outside of time
and is like any other fairy tale, any other nightgown brushing against the peak
of wine-drenched rooftops in the borderless villages of my dreams: easy to believe.

No milkmaids, angels, or yellow-vested painters in my childhood, Chagall. Chagall, Chagall
    . . . an empty easel chair.
We descend together into a rainstorm at so-many-thousand feet,
and the Eiffel Tower tears at the belly of the plane
because it needs to be there. Landing gear, luggage, plastic cabinets fall in order as we
    float away

over my neighbor's side-lot—its triangular shape safeguarding the presence of frozen cats
    and fruit trees.
It's good to see it again. It's good to see it differently.
Chagall, push over, make room for me. I have seven fingers too,
each wrapped tightly around the crabapple melting in my palm.

MIDWINTER RAINS OVER MONTRÉAL:
A VIDEO INSTALLATION

Hold this poem very still, so that it may be the fixed point by which we'll measure the velocity
of rain descending on the frozen St. Lawrence River. Soon, a young skater in a blue tuque
will glide amid a group of fathers pushing strollers in circles around adolescent girls

practicing two-foot spins until grace glows from their skin; their older brothers,
briefly released from the plastic and Plexiglas of the hockey rink, will race for miles, through exhaustion,
from beneath the highway overpass toward the smoking Molson brewery on the horizon.

The river thickens throughout the winter, though snow limits the occasion for skating
much of the season. A hard midwinter rain like this one, and then its end, sends families down
the cobbled streets to gather on the banks, and skate the natural surface washed clean.

They are not all characters from the *Saturday Evening Post*: scarves extending sideways from stupid
smiles; some Québécois youth, like drunken men and boys from a Bruegel painting, who strap
flattened foreleg bones of reindeer to their feet, will skate at full speed into their best friends' bodies.

SELF-PORTRAIT WITH SEVEN FINGERS II

The first thing I ever saw was a trough. Simple, square, half hollow, half oval. A market trough.
MARC CHAGALL

And the first thing I remember, Chagall, was daylight.
In fact, dust. Particles of dust swirling in the daylight coming through the bedroom
    window.

The light was still because the dust was dancing in it.

I could still look at it in wonder, too dumb to doubt its charity.
Like the promise of air holding parachute silk high above the children's heads in the park,
or water overflowing, pushing out the ripples, becoming like glass, before it falls.

We are like this, you and I, the trough, and the light and dust inside.

SUMMERTIME (1943)

Although I don't detect the slightest breeze by looking at you, I can see the wide
outline of your right thigh (even the faint hue of flesh mixing with the almost-blue of
    your dress)
as you stand on the cement steps and wait, for whom?
Screenless and open over your right shoulder, the shade half-drawn on the lives inside

mirrors the hat brim casting a shadow over your eyes. The first-floor window
looks out onto a sidewalk with no treebelt, and reflects the noontime sun in such a way
it reminds me of Main Street and Liberty, in Springfield, Massachusetts,
and of a tale I heard too many times as a child, about my *pépé*, François, who,

when living across from the bus station, used to urinate out of his first-floor living room
    window
while the pigeons pecked at rotten chicken and exhaust clung to tenement awnings;
and once, deep into an afternoon drunk, the neighbors left their rain-slicked rubbers
out on the sidewalk to dry, and François filled them up. For some reason,

the sidewalk around you is completely clean, calling attention to the fact that this is a
    Hopper painting,
not Springfield. Though you do stand perfectly composed in your isolation,
the fan on inside the window promises an occupant within. And though your hat may
    suggest otherwise,
there is no slip beneath your cotton day dress, telling me you might be waiting on a man
    like Frank

SCENES FROM A VILLAGE: A TRIPTYCH

Or, "They retained a bias for deductive reasoning that distinguished them from English-speaking newcomers."

We spent the better part of the afternoon scrubbing his brains from the wallboards. After the clerics caught wind that it was a suicide, the police arrived at the house to apprehend the body and force it to stand trial. The jury commenced before supper and evening prayer, finding the corpse guilty of self-murder. They dragged him out into the square and flogged him one hundred times across his stripped-bare back. Skin split but nothing dripped out. Papa's head just hung heavy from the rack they flung him over. His head cracked by birdshot like the watermelon I accidentally dropped last summer. They sent a clear message to all: no one escapes God's law.

Or, "By self-examination, the pious always found failings
in their own conduct to be confessed and expiated."

Because some part of human flesh is always left sticking to spirit, self-punishment was the only fit penance for the widow's lack of perfection. Exile from family and friends: sleepless nights on the cold ground of animal pens, shuffling around the village square in corn husk shoes, iron-studded belts turned inward—tightened, wormwood added to overpower the unintended pleasure in food, swallowing phlegm of diseased drunks dying of bedsores in poorhouse and work farm shacks. She envied the missionary priests above all, captured and beheaded by Huron insurgents. And her self-punishment was most ruthless for this lust of martyrdom.

Each firefly blinking above the marsh: the lost soul of an unbaptized infant. Limbo in frontier, frontier in limbo. Englishmen who go there lately after dark with instruments and jars say they're not fireflies at all, but luminescent gas rising from beneath the wasteland. Further proof they're damned souls, I say. Visions of a canoe, crown of fire floating in the sky above! A baby crying from inside his mother's womb. Last week, the sun disappeared behind the moon. Light shone out like a halo. I repeat my prayers three times backwards whenever I leave the house: Me upon mercy have God, me upon mercy have God, me upon mercy have God.

ORIZURU

At the kitchen table, you wince when taking a sip of the cheap red wine—
telling me, in the clearest way you know, that it's too harsh. I'm always a few steps
     behind, as I correct
each mistake and refold toward an already-lost perfection. In the extra minutes before
     the buses
arrived, my sixth grade class folded cranes to send to an imagined memorial in Japan.

The assignment worked, if the purpose was to place in the mind of each child
     a distant city
of suffering: of fabric burning patterns into flesh, of mother and child—hand in hand—
becoming silhouettes of ash on a sidewalk. Nagasaki, your neighbor city, is beautiful,
you tell me: a city of white, surrounded by ocean and hills. Like San Francisco.

With its own history of fire. For the time I lived at 32nd and Geary, my fireplace
     remained empty.
And now I wish I'd filled it with these white paper birds, in memoriam, or, at least,
as a series of small steps toward a peace I didn't know how to get nearer to.
The proper way, you say, is to leave the wings unfolded, so that the wish will stay within,

and with a needle, thread the tiny hole in its belly, push the steel through the empty
     space
inside, and pierce the thin back, until every one of the thousand is linked, unwished.
Tilting to the side on its one bent wing, as if leaning against yours for support,
my crane is lined with unnecessary creases. You can't decide whether to keep it there
     or pull away.

AFTER WE DISEMBARK AND SPEND THE DAY ON THE ISLAND WHILE THE SHIP'S REPAIRED, I BOARD ALONE, FLIP THROUGH A CHINESE RESTAURANT CALENDAR, AND WRITE THREE POEMS TO EXPRESS MY FEELINGS

(i)

Toward the tattered top edge of the "endless" scroll painting,
a man leading a horse up a winding mountain trail

fades into mist. The horse's hindquarters less obscure
than the thin stroke of rope around its neck, the invisible hand

grasping the other end. Ming Dynasty masters were experts at
whatever is the opposite of shade, a white vapor fade washes

victims into the underside of the paper. Even mist seems to vanish
into deeper mist. When Tang Yin was left in the summer

of 1508, he wrote thirty-nine farewell poems, of which nineteen
survive. Economy of ink, a quality saved for his paintings:

a mare a mere three strokes: it's easy to imagine how a script
and calligraphy might grow out of such strict reductionism.

I want to ask you if it's still pictographic if the horse comes
to signify *Grace*, *Endurance*, or *Speed*. What if the meaning

turns to *Mist*? Not what the horse embodies or exudes,
but the condition of the clearing where the horse now exists.

(ii)

When we boarded the corroded ship, we were surprised to find
an infant asleep atop a crate of clementines, in third-class,

in the hollow hull full of carpet-covered skids, stinking
from fifty years of sprawled bodies, heads propped on luggage.

With just one book, we read Rimbaud's letters to his family
to each other in a language I doubt anyone understood,

including him: *I don't intend to stay here long; soon I will
know when I'm leaving. I did not find . . .* What? Paradise?

Who can believe in it? That Welsh guy who bought a cabana bar
and married the lady who came with it had jaundiced eyes

and a five-year-old who was uncomfortably comfortable
with strangers—creeping behind my stool to stroke my thigh

and climb on my lap five minutes after we got there.
There's their tradeoff. What else do I remember of the beach?

Your dark basement. Your memories sitting at the woodstove
with your father on Friday nights, burning a week's worth of trash.

(iii)

They're called "ghost paintings," when, for easy cash or to help
a friend, an artist signs his own name to a known forgery.

They were usually painted by an apprentice or close friend,
so does it matter if he wasn't actually on the scene, as long as

he knows of the vista, and the way lightning strikes
like a jagged question mark, as one sits alone by a window,

moistening the inkstone and chewing on a brush, before composing
eight couplets to express an unclear feeling? Does it matter

that *dong dweiji* means shit pig, when we sit at a propane grill
for our last meal, and the waitress tells us it's "black pork"

and neglects to add that the pigs feed on human waste
from the bottoms of outhouses on small farms in the hills?

Pigs eat shit everywhere. A horse leads or is led, leaves or is left.
And my memory of you shrinking on shore is your memory too,

of watching from the top deck, or going below to nap, or
counting rat droppings, or apple seeds, next to the engine room.

SELF-PORTRAIT WITH SEVEN FINGERS III

While in France I took part in this unique revolution of artistic technique, in my thoughts—I might even say, in my soul—I returned to my own land. I lived with my back toward what lay before me.

MARC CHAGALL

Planet, Chagall, in Greek means *Wanderer*.
Whenever we turn from home, like the earth turning from the sun, we begin our way
    toward it again.
The window open over your shoulder, for instance, might reveal
a field of wheat, a steeple, and a rusted train rumbling toward
heaps of scrap metal on the horizon.
To chart the passage, compass and wind rose alone will not do.

Some landmasses must be stretched and some memories distorted
to make drunk the course leading to our respective points of origin.
Not every celestial body needs to clumsily orbit
a sun that turns blood red
                    and kilns the solar system before turning to dust inside.
And in the next life, Chagall, we will neither reflect nor emit light.
We will travel like dark matter, and move in all directions at once.

THE MADONNA AND CHILD WITH ST. ANNE

The original hangs in the Uffizi Gallery in Florence, Italy.

But I've never been there, and neither has my grandfather.

There's a reproduction at the entrance of the outdoor shrine where we walk the Stations of the Cross.

Where a brown recluse hangs from a henchman's club.

Where fire ants race across the freshly lacquered legs of martyrs.

"He suffered," my grandfather says. With empty lungs: "Oh, how they made him suffer."

Jesus looks like a murderballer—his neck sunk into a muscle-bound torso, legs shriveled like they've been confined to a wheelchair for thirty-three years.

"Beautiful," he says. "That man was beautiful."

During the plague, orphans ran circles around Masaccio's house, shaking the tibia of a dog yanked to pieces in the gutter.

Past the X'ed-out sign of the cobbler, past the pile of hearts and guts the butcher left simmering in the sun.

All day the kids roll dice against the worn street curb, talking shit about God.

At Station 6 my grandfather wipes cobwebs off Veronica wiping sweat off the face of Jesus.

He offers me the prayer book he can no longer read if we hurry, if I take him home *immediately*.

He thinks his grandson—my cousin—is sleeping with his wife.

Men arrive at Masaccio's studio dressed as crows.

Men swing open heavy curtains and closed shutters, their hollow beaks stuffed with sun-dried juniper and cloves.

Sunlight pools on bloody vomit and a body of boils blooming outward from below the balls.

Purple peonies float like bruises around Station 14.

"The Tomb," my grandfather says to fallen linen. "Let's go."

Past the Magic Lantern strip club on the drive home, he repeats those stories as if from rote memory.

Folks down from Maine fifty years ago, and this one girl puts her hairless touchhole right in his face and makes it pucker.

He demonstrates the contraction with index finger and thumb as if it were yesterday.

The wood panel of the Virgin hasn't always been in a museum.

The story goes, "The Madonna and Child with St. Anne" hung in the nuns' parlor at St. Ambrogio Church in Florence.

Then the story ends.

I think the stripper must be dead by now.

No one knows how it got from there to the Uffizi Gallery, or all the places it might have gone in between.

His oldest daughter pulled to the side of a country road once and made a pass at him, he tells me as we wait in the Burger King drive-thru.

"I don't know. Years ago."

He swears it's true.

With a nosegay in a death-grip, Masaccio is removed from his studio by men in the black robes of crows.

He thinks they want him to die so they can videotape their orgies.

It's only me and the ghosts in the basement that are on his side, "Right?"

The kids shout for "just a twig" of the dead man's flowers.

I'm surprised "pucker" is still in his vocabulary, but not a bit by "touchhole."

Action verbs are the first to go, but no one notices with how we talk around them.

"Pick it up," the old man says while balancing fries in his lap.

Roman sandals are only obstacles to be crossed over.

The cupped hands of a savior are only a chamber to soothe, or further terrify, a nervous bird heart.

The orphans' dice are carved from the bones of road kill.

The tibia from an abandoned dog is the same length as an angel's spine.

He hides the keys before bed now and holds his sleeping pill under his tongue.

"Faster," he says.

When pine needles brown and fall around the Stations of the Cross.

When hoarfrost forms on bent knees.

When snow piles on Pilate's head like a skullcap.

We won't be there to see it.

One of the orphans rolls snake eyes.

They say he was the first painter to depict natural light.

We roll through the last three stop signs.

I'm on your side, I say.

SELF-PORTRAIT IN SHOCK

I've heard the experts argue that the term should be discarded, since there is no such
    thing as treatment,
rather, only the treatment of its causes—the effect of the simple expectation that your legs
    will stay
forever beneath you; that your L7 and L8 vertebrae will not pop and shatter like Corelle
    teacups
meeting the kitchen floor; that you will, one day, stand again at the edge of a frozen lake,
    naming
the stars after poor neighborhoods you passed through: Moran-yuk, the Mission District,
the North End, Hungry Hill . . . ; that you will not find your only child floating facedown
in the neighbor's swimming pool, for the first time not pretending he's dead: water
    heavies his lungs
as your lover suns herself on the deck, tumors ripening in her breasts like Red Flame
    grapes—
which is why I study these moments, meditate on them like the Catholic nuns at my
    childhood parish,
who dared to enter the fourteen tiny and painful worlds of carved wood between stained
    glass—
as I stood in a line of clip-on neckties and starched pants, making up sins to confess.

THE LAST PAINTING (OR, SOME MORE ABOUT CROWS)

Anyone who's filled a page with wings knows the pleasure
of constructing depth. But who can tell just by looking whether

the birds move toward us or away? The hardened oil of van Gogh's
Wheatfield with Crows reveals three distinct movements:

one, the upward flick of the wrist; two, a retraction of the fingers—like
the slight, abrupt almost-collapse of a metal tent frame that kids

play camp games beneath; and three, the final, downward slope
that completes each bird into its rounded, flattened "M" shape.

A painting is an artifact of movement. The cast of a private dance
scholars spend their careers analyzing, grabbing at each crow midair

and flipping it forward and back in order to prove one theory
or another. Still, each stroke is a distinct spasm issued from

a steadied body. Her body is so still when I enter the cafeteria
for visiting hours, at first I think she's crying; her head down

deep in concentration, as I get closer I see she's just painting.
"Some birds are close," my sister says, "and some are far away."

When she pauses at the apex of a "W" to look up at me and then
her therapist, none of us know whether it's a tail or a beak being

pressed into existence. And when she shares the accompanying
story, about the time we scared four crows from a bare tree

in an empty field, she leaves me out. It's her story. And she wants
to be the type of person who goes to such places alone. It's her

idea to turn off the dirt road, to run through the dead grass
waving her arms in the air and screaming to the sky as if for rescue.

She sees the birds lift, heavy and deliberate and in unison, to fly
to the edge of the woods and warn others in the area of Danger.

"I can't go back there," she says to her therapist (or to me),
"They say a crow will remember a person's face for years."

IV.
THE CULT POEM

THE CULT POEM

(i)

Apaches pass over the intramural soccer game between Indonesia and France.

France starts two Irishmen, a Kiwi, and a Spanish sweeper. Three Filipinos and a Somali play for Indonesia, but the crowd doesn't mention a thing

as the helicopters brush up against the no-fly zone

then circle back over the fields again.

Hello.

My brainwashing officially began with "Hey Jude" dubbed over video footage of beautiful girls boarding a chartered bus.

The camera zoomed in on a flashed peace sign as the door folded shut behind the last in line.

The young woman beside me in the auditorium caressed my hand all through the Malaysian dance performance. The traditional tea ceremony. The Ambassador of Peace Awards.

Unwrapping a thin stick of pink chewing gum and placing it on my tongue

while a drunken Newfie slurred into the mike: "This organization's great, right? I just heardd'ya guys this morning, and today . . . *I'm* an Am*bass* . . ."

The PA system cuts out.

(ii)

If you want to go global, best to start a cultural-exchange division to help bring in members from all over the world.

Best to seek out someone able to translate precepts and parables into easy-to-comprehend English.

That's where I come in.

Not every member will have the task of standing on a subway platform stabbing a plastic bag of poisonous gas with the tip of his umbrella.

Not every member will be asked to kneel in the damp grass of a darkened athletic field

performing fellatio in her cheerleading outfit while the crowd inside begins a moving rendition of "Give Peace a Chance."

We don't all have the legs or moral dexterity to be the physical embodiment of our Divine Leader.

Some talents are more subtle. Some connections less obvious. Like the importance of white teeth.

They are better for smiling a healthy greeting.

Hello.

Hello, again.

(iii)
It's really not what you think. Some of us live in our own, far away from the hidden compound in the hills.

We work nine-to-five jobs and have genuine interests outside of apocalypse.

I collect newspaper clippings on American death-row inmates.

This one's scheduled to die in Enfield, Connecticut, on the same day as our next attack.

But I have to get back to work.

The Homecoming

Alone, you get lost in your loneliness—
wandering in the night like a cold wind
blowing across the frozen tundra.

Members of our Chemical Brigade sink into subway tunnels the same way governments sink the hollowed needle-tip of a syringe

into the veins of those whose names I tape to the wall above my writing desk.

(iv)
Because American death is clean, clinical.
Because American death is civilized.

After a doctor assesses the condemned's veins,
the Restraint Team protects the arms
in a holding cell next to the death chamber
while the Operations Team inspects the injection apparatus.

Catheters are inserted into each arm of the body
strapped to the gurney. Two, in case the first one clogs.

Everyone retreats from the room and the superintendent
uses a light switch to signal the executioner, who stands
in a separate room housing the syringe system.

100 cc of sodium pentothal for unconsciousness,
150 cc of Pavulon to paralyze the muscles,
and 150 cc of potassium chloride to kill the heart,
while everyone stands behind a mirrored window—
as if to remind the victim that *he* is the one responsible,
just he and machinery.

I wonder,
what if they skipped the first step? For how long
is the brain conscious of its impending death?
That is panic in its purest sense.

When my own sternum tightens
thoughts turn to heart failure,
then to the brain's lack of oxygen.

Blood backs into our lungs as the last
bits of energy burn to naught constructing
the countdown formula forming in my head.
"This is it? *This* is the place?"
Because we all go somewhere.
And somehow.

3,000 will die because of house fires.
15,000 will fall to their ends. And some smaller number
must fit into both those categories.

30 percent to heart disease. 23 to cancer.
3 to Alzheimer's. A grandfather,
for instance, remembers just enough to be
too hard on himself. And to remind you
he's forgotten more than you'll ever know.
A lucky guess if he could tell you the color
of the room in which he goes. He'll sooner
forget how to swallow.

How many will share the final vision of taillights
disappearing down a rain-slicked road?

~~Roberts~~
~~Pursuley~~
~~Richmond~~
~~Miller~~
Ross

> *There were always tears in your heart.*
> *Even at the moment of fiercest determination,*
> *you were restless with despair.*

Yellow. The room will be yellow.

(v)

Two control rooms flank some death chambers.

When the light turns on, each operator flicks his respective switch: sodium pentothal,
Pavulon, potassium chloride.

Both computers, however, immediately erase their histories from their hard drives.

There's no way of knowing which operator, or which syringe system, was responsible.

The implication is strange, like the actions of a murderously deep sleepwalker, or some-
one in an alcohol-induced blackout:

constant anxiety over something missing.

And someone is always missing.

(vi)

> *But in a cabin in the driving snow,*
> *a man waits—he, too, alone—*
> *watching you approach, cold.*

Michael Ross receives injections of Depro-Lupron once a month to make him come to
terms with what he's done.

Now he spends his days in his cell writing letters to the victims' families.

24, 16, 17, 23.

Lack of testosterone has caused his breasts to grow like a woman's.

But since he's on suicide watch, they won't let him wear a bra.

19, 14, 14, 17 years old.

He's cancelled all his appeals

and has sent a revised request to the kitchen for his last meal: a Burger King double cheeseburger, SpaghettiOs, and half a pumpkin pie.

(vii)

The first step in mind control is behavior control. We begin by inviting the candidate to something he wouldn't mind doing normally.

Say, "Join us for a day hike." Or, "Come to our international soccer tournament."

If you can fill the individual's calendar with activities he enjoys, you minimize the leisure time he once spent on his own.

A common misconception is that the "brainwashed" don't know it. How could anyone who has undergone such a fundamental change in personality and outlook on life not realize it?

They prefer to think of it as a "spiritual awakening," or simply a life *choice* that has made them happier than whatever was forced on them by parents, neighbors, peers, and institutions.

What, after all, is the alternative to feeling that most of the important decisions you've made have been wrong?

I've been in dive bars full of those

who stumble home to wrap sheets that haven't been washed in two years around themselves and half-naked strangers.

The one action we hope will fuse us to the present after the present tense has been lost to us.

Might as well surrender your mind to someone who knows better what to do with it.

Trust in the Divine Leader to make decisions for you.

Michael Ross grew up on a farm strangling chickens and wound up raping and asphyxiating young women.

His initial request of a lobster and a dozen steamers was denied.

(viii)

For the last week ex-girlfriends have been feeding me drinks in my dreams—

Kate, Sarah, Sarah, Rachel—teaching me to distinguish between guilt, shame, dread, and remorse.
All relationships must be approved before they can be considered "fulfilling."
I'm still single.

> *As you step onto the porch,*
> *he waits for you to turn the handle*
> *and open the door . . . of his heart.*

(ix)

Remember the news story?

About the four youths who abducted and held captive a high school sophomore for thirty-nine days?

They beat her, raped her, made her drink her own urine, and then forced her to call home to tell her parents she was "with friends" and "okay."

The trial revealed that over a hundred people knew she was being held prisoner in that basement.

Classmates stopped by to take turns, to put cigarettes out on her flesh until she begged them for death, to just "get it over with."

Instead, they lit firecrackers off in her vagina—the wick sticking out like the string of a tampon.

Imagine being forced to live in that moment just prior to the flick of the lighter.

The cause of death was determined to be shock: a result of immolation with butane and fire.

They found her corpse in a fifty-five-gallon drum.

The metal protecting it against the landfill pressing in.

(x)

Perhaps it's possible to live on within any structure,
with the smallest particles of our being.

But first we must die.

We can live on, maybe even
inside the chemical structure of a poison,
or a poem.
Sodium pentothal is a symmetrical block
of empty squares, like an apartment complex
where I spent my days
watching the shadows of crows
pass above a frosted glass roof.
Michael Ross will live
in the right rear chamber. A corner studio
apartment with a view of the river
where three orange neon crosses
reflect off the water every night.

> *He's been there a long time,*
> *waiting just inside the door,*
> *expecting you to come alone, and knock.*

Victims of our Chemical Brigade exist in $C_4H_{10}FO_2P$.
I can't make sense of it,
but I hope they find peace
within its strict rules.

If I live on, it will be
in the architecture of words
arranged in lines

like suburban houses
dotting a dead-end street:
the nouns, colonials;
adjectives, ranches; and verbs,
the common, trusty cape.

(xi)

Michael Ross has changed his mind again
and has just released a statement saying
he prefers to die with an empty stomach.

(xii)

Perillos of Athens invented an execution device not very different from an elaborate drum
oven. He called it the "Brazen Cow."

Cast entirely of brass, a fire was set beneath to slowly roast the victim inside.

A system of tubes in the bull's head transformed the roasting man's screams into a low-sounding *moo*.

Incensed smoke puffed out the ears to keep from spoiling the emperor's feasts.
When the door on the side of the cow was opened, the remains were said to have shone like a pile of jewels.

The bones were then couriered to an artisan and made into bracelets.
 (xiii)

Countries today are no different. America has a larger percentage of its population in prison than any other.

China kills the most citizens

but no laws require accurate records or reporting.

Families in impoverished villages hang onto hope that their loved ones will one day return

as opportunistic jewelers remove firing squad slugs from their relatives' bodies and solder them to necklace chains.

Some say there is no better way to show devotion to the government, and your trust in the righteousness of its choices, than to wear one of these around your neck.

Studies have shown jewelry reinforces—and, in some instances, may even advance— one's status within the group.

Studies have shown that bright-colored clothes make people appear happier and more trustworthy.

But it's our sleeping patterns that define us.

That's why the Divine Leader's video-stream sermon is scheduled for 4:30 sharp every Tuesday, Thursday, and Sunday morning.

Some countries deny their citizens sleep.

Some require them to stand until their kidneys fail.

Some countries drag their citizens into the streets, break their legs with baseball bats, and douse their bodies with kerosene.

By slow starvation, forced labor, and leg chains;

by rape and mutilation; by shock of cattle prod; acid drip; and slow asphyxiation;

by bodies stretched upon a ladder; by broken bottles in the anus,

some countries make their citizens beg for death.

100,000 of us will be tortured this year. 2,200 prior to execution.

Michael Ross's last words were "No, thank you."

Some countries wrap their citizens in tarps and dump their bodies into unmarked graves.

Don't be afraid.
Open the door.
Lean on him.
Feel a warmth like the sun
rising to meet you in the morning.

(xiv)

The snow has thawed in the hill towns and summer is almost here.

When the souls of those who are saved will gather at the shipyards and sail home.

Will you walk with me at dawn to the docks to greet them?

Will you feast with us after the soccer tournament? (France is a shoo-in, after all.)

Will you burn the boats at dusk and watch the souls ascend in smoke?

We choose you. Will you choose us?

NOTES

The epigraph for "About Crows" is from Lawrence Raab's "Other Children."

Section three of "An Alternate History of Enfield, Mass." is based on accounts from *Quabbin: A History and Explorers Guide* by Michael Tougias.

Passages in section three of "Five Memories of Motion" are from Auguste Deter's medical file, discovered in 1995 in the archives at the University of Frankfurt.

In "A River," the lines "Under the frozen river the other river flows / on its side in the dark" are from Jorie Graham's poem "History." In the same poem, "the dark light of the eye" and language about molecule breakdown in the eyeball is from James Elkin's essay "How to Look at Darkness."

The Marc Chagall quotes at the start of "Self-Portrait with Seven Fingers I, II, and III" are from his book *My Life*.

The epigraphs and miscellaneous details for "Scenes from a Village: A Triptych" are from Peter Moogk's *La Nouvelle France: The Making of French Canada—A Cultural History*.

Research for "The Cult Poem" centered largely on the Aum Shinrikyo sarin gas attacks in Tokyo, Japan, as well as Amnesty International's *Torture Worldwide: An Affront to Human Dignity*, and various other sources gathered from the stacks of Wichita State University's Ablah Library.

Reunion • Fleda Brown
Linda Gregerson, Judge, 2007

The Royal Baker's Daughter • Barbara Goldberg
David St. John, Judge, 2008

Falling Brick Kills Local Man • Mark Kraushaar
Marilyn Nelson, Judge, 2009

The Lightning That Strikes the Neighbors' House • Nick Lantz
Robert Pinsky, Judge, 2010

Last Seen • Jacqueline Jones LaMon
Cornelius Eady, Judge, 2011

Voodoo Inverso • Mark Wagenaar
Jean Valentine, Judge, 2012

About Crows • Craig Blais
Terrance Hayes, Judge, 2013